MONSTER

FRUIT TREES

AuthorHouse™
1663 Liberty Drive
Bloomington, IN 47403
www.authorhouse.com
Phone: 833-262-8899

This book is printed on acid-free paper.

ISBN: 978-1-6655-1588-7 (sc)
ISBN: 978-1-6655-1589-4 (e)

Library of Congress Control Number: 2021902114

Print information available on the last page.

Published by AuthorHouse 02/09/2021

authorHOUSE®

MONSTER
FRUIT TREES

MONSTER FRUIT
Cedar Sapp
Orange Juice * Almond Joy
Banana Boat
Apple Jack * Grape Nuts
Grapefruit Squeezie

RUBY BURCHETTE

Monster Fruit
Next, Orange Juice, how's
your squeeze?
Is your juice sweet or tingly?

Orange Juice
Sir, my skin is too thick and hard to
squeeze. What can you advise me to do
to have a thinner skin?

Monster Fruit
Oh my! That's a difficult ques-
tion. Let me do some research
on it and get back to you.
Okay?

Orange Juice
Sure! I'll keep spraying my
roots twice a day!

Monster Fruit
Sounds good to me!

Cedar Sapp
Orange Juice, I hope my sap
is not streaming over on your trunk.

Orange Juice
No! I haven't seen any sap
flowing near my area.

Cedar Sapp
Just let me know if you
see any signs, okay?

Monster Fruit
Hey Apple Jack...how plentiful are you; and will you be ready for Halloween so kids can do "apple-bobbing?" You know that's their famous time of the winter.

Apple Jack
But of course... we are sprouting like crazy. The only concern I have is how many reds I can produce. Not too many kids like my greens.

Monster Fruit
WOW! I had no idea that there was a preference for the occasion.

Apple Jack
Oh yes... there is. However, I can use my greens for juice for the older people.

Monster Fruit
Hey Banana Boat... I didn't forget you. Give me an update on your production.

Monster Fruit
You're right Banana Boat. It was always encouraging people that breakfast is the most important meal of the day. Times are changing.

Banana Boat
Well... we are growing slow. Although we all know that I am a great product for breakfast cereal, a lot of people are skipping breakfast. Some say they are 'fasting' and just eating lunch and dinner.

Grapes Nuts
It can work if you blend me with Banana Boat, and we can come up with a juicy name.

Monster Fruit
Banana Boat, I think that is genius. What does everyone think about this invention?

Banana Boat
Yes they are. I'm gonna have to be creative with a commercial to attract people back to me. I know I can be bruised if I sit around too long. Oh! How about putting me in a blender for a quick 'shake-like' digestible meal?

Banana Boat
Oh now... you want to capitalize on my product.

Grapes Nuts
Not really... I was thinking we can merge together and make a greater profit with people to choose between you and me. It's called "partnership for profit." (Applause break-out).

Monster Fruit
Golly ghee... let me jump in here. I agree with Grapes Nuts. I've never heard of bananas and grapes as an associated ingredient. I think you're right Grapes Nuts. I think there could be a greater demand if you two partner-up.

Monster Fruit
Okay everyone, let's table this meeting until next week. Perhaps each of you could have a more productive report. All agree? (All trees bowed). Cedar Sapp... we will determine why you are dripping so much... okay?

Monster Fruit
To you Grapefruit Squeezie... marketing you in different facilities would profit you a lot. Who can deny you? (Ha! Ha!)

Cedar Sapp
Yes! Sounds good.

Grapefruit Squeezie
Thank you Monster Fruit for having confidence in me.

Monster Fruit
Banana Boat and Grapes Nuts... partnership equals great profits... don't be hating.

Monster Fruit
Orange Juice and Apple Jack... teaming-up to package-up is beneficial, as people can preserve you without waste. Until tomorrow, sleep well all of you. See you tomorrow.

Monster Fruit

Cedar Sapp

Orange Juice

Almond Joy

Apple Jack

Banana Boat

Grape Nuts

Grapefruit Squeezie

Printed in the United States
By Bookmasters